Occult or Exact Science?

By Helena P. Blavatsky

Copyright © 2021 Lamp of Trismegistus. All rights reserved. No part of this publication may be reproduced or transmitted in any form or by any means, electronic or mechanical, including photocopying, recording, or by any information storage and retrieval system, without permission in writing from Lamp of Trismegistus. Reviewers may quote brief passages.

ISBN: 978-1-63118-578-6

Esoteric Classics

Other Books in this Series and Related Titles

Aurora of the Philosophers by Paracelsus (978-1-63118-507-6)

Clairvoyance and Psychic Abilities by A Besant &c (978-1-63118-403-1)

The Feminine Occult by various authors (978-1-63118-711-7)

Rosicrucian Rules, Secret Signs, Codes and Symbols by various (978-1-63118-488-8)

An Outline of Theosophy by C W Leadbeater (978-1-63118-452-9)

Paracelsus, the Four Elements and Their Spirits by M P Hall (978-1-63118-400-0)

Essays on Ancient Magic by Helena P Blavatsky (978-1-63118-535-9)

Essays on the Esoteric Tradition of Karma by A Besant &c (978-1-63118-426-0)

The Use of Evil by Annie Besant (978-1-63118-532-8)

The Alchemical Catechism of Paracelsus by Paracelsus (978-1-63118-513-7)

Alchemy in the Nineteenth Century by Helena P Blavatsky (978-1-63118-446-8)

Qabbalistic Teachings and the Tree of Life by M P Hall (978-1-63118-482-6)

The Historic, Mythic and Mystic Christ by Annie Besant (978–1–63118–533–5)

The Hidden Mysteries of Christianity by Annie Besant (978–1–63118–534–2)

History, Analysis and Secret Tradition of the Tarot by Hall &c (978-1-63118-445-1)

Crystal Vision Through Crystal Gazing by Frater Achad (978-1-63118-455-0)

The Golden Verses of Pythagoras: Five Translations (978-1-63118-479-6)

Arcane Formulas or Mental Alchemy by W W Atkinson (978-1-63118-459-8)

The Machinery of the Mind by Dion Fortune (978-1-63118-451-2)

The A E Waite Reader: A Selection of Occult Essays (978-1-63118-515-1)

The Leadbeater Reader: A Selection of Occult Essays (978-1-63118-483-3)

Audio versions are also available on Audible, Amazon and Apple

Other Books in this Series and Related Titles

Occultism, Semi-Occultism & Pseudo Occultism by A Besant (978–1–63118–577–9)

The Fourth-Gospel and Synoptical Problem by G R S Mead (978–1–63118–576–2)

On the Bhagavad-Gita by T Subba Row &c (978–1–63118–575–5)

What Theosophy Does for Us by C W Leadbeater (978–1–63118–574–8)

Spiritual Life for Man by Annie Besant (978–1–63118–573–1)

The Mysteries by Annie Besant (978–1–63118–572–4)

Fundamental Ideas of Theosophy by Bhagwan Das (978–1–63118–571–7)

Dreams: What They Are and Caused by C W Leadbeater (978–1–63118–570–0)

Communication Between Different Worlds by Annie Besant (978–1–63118–569–4)

Animism, Magic and the Omnipotence of Thought by S Freud (978–1–63118–568–7)

Buddhism by F Otto Schrader (978–1–63118–567–0)

Death by W W Westcott (978–1–63118–566–3)

The Religion of Theosophy by Bhagwan Das (978–1–63118–565–6)

The Spirit of Zoroastrianism by Henry S Olcott (978–1–63118–564–9)

The Brotherhood of Religions by Annie Besant (978–1–63118–563–2)

Fourth Book of Maccabees by Josephus (978-1-63118-562-5)

The Story of Ahikar by Ahiqar (978-1-63118-561-8)

Vision of the Spirit by C. Jinarajadasa (978-1-63118-560-1)

Occult Arts by William Q. Judge (978-1-63118-559-5)

Kali the Mother by Sister Nivedita (978-1-63118-558-8)

Love and Death by Sri Aurobindo (978–1–63118–557–1)

Audio versions are also available on Audible, Amazon and Apple

Table of Contents

Introduction...7

Part I...9

Part II...27

INTRODUCTION

The word "esoteric" can be difficult to define. Esotericism in general can be seen less as a system of beliefs and more as a category, which encompasses numerous, different systems of beliefs. It's a bit of juxtaposition, since the word "esoteric" indicates something that few people know about, while the term itself broadly covers numerous philosophies, practices, areas of study and belief systems.

In a greater sense, Esotericism acts as a storehouse for secret knowledge, which is often considered ancient (by *tradition, if not by fact),* passed down from generation to generation, in private. At various times in history, simply possessing the knowledge of some of these subjects, was considered illegal and a jailable offence, if discovered. This usually included such general topics as Alchemy, Pharmacology, Qabalah, Hermeticism, Occultism, Ceremonial Magic, Astrology, Divination, Rosicrucianism and so on. Collectively, these areas of study were often referred to as the esoteric sciences.

Sometimes, the outer garment of a subject isn't esoteric, while what is hidden beneath it, is. As an example, Freemasonry isn't necessarily esoteric by nature (at *least not anymore),* but certain signs, passwords and handshakes given to the candidate during their initiation, are in fact, esoteric, in the sense that they are hidden from the general public.

Today, in the twenty-first century, such topics are readily available at bookstores across the country, and numerous mainsteam publishers offer beginners guides and coffee-table volumes on many of these subjects, intended for mass appeal. Books like *"The Secret"* have turned previously arcane topics into household knowledge. All that being the case, however, it isn't to say that there still aren't buried secrets to uncover, ancient wisdom being ignored and forgotten mysteries to be explored. In fact, it is often that we are only able to further our own studies by standing on the shoulders of these disappearing giants.

Lamp of Trismegistus is doing its part to help preserve humanity's esoteric history by making some of these classics available to those students who are seeking to unearth the knowledge of these ancient colossi.

So, be sure to check other titles from our *Esoteric Classics* series, as well as our *Occult Fiction, Theosophical Classics, Foundations of Freemasonry Series, Supernatural Fiction, Paranormal Research Series, Studies in Buddhism* and our *Christian Apocrypha Series.* You can also download the audio versions of most of these titles from Amazon, Apple or Audible, for learning on the go.

OCCULT OR EXACT SCIENCE?

PART I

Ecce signum! Behold the sign foreseen in a brighter future; the problem that will be *the* question of the forthcoming age, that every thoughtful, earnest father will be asking himself with regard to his children's education in the 20th century. And let it be stated at once, that by "Occult Science" neither *the life* of a *chela* nor the austerities of an ascetic are here meant; but simply the study of that which alone can furnish the key to the mysteries of nature, and unveil the problems of the universe and of psycho-physical man—even though one should not feel inclined to go any deeper.

Every new discovery made by modern science vindicates the truths of the archaic philosophy. The true occultist is acquainted with no single problem that esoteric science is unable to solve, if approached in the right direction; the scientific bodies of the West have as yet no phenomenon of natural science that they can fathom to its innermost depths, or explain in all its aspects. Exact science fails to do so—in *this* cycle, for reasons that will be given further on. Nevertheless the pride of the age, which revolts against the intrusion into the empire of science of old especially of transcendental—truths, is growing every year more intolerant. Soon the world will behold it soaring in the clouds of self-sufficiency like a new tower of Babel, to share, perchance, the fate of the Biblical monument.

In a recent scientific work on Anthropology,[1] one can read the following: "It is then given to us, at last, *to know* (?), to grasp, to

---

[1] *Bulletin de la Société d'Anthropologie*, 3e fascic., p. 384.

handle and measure the forces through which it is claimed, that God proceeded. . . . . We have made electricity our postman, light our draughts-man, affinity our journeyman," etc., etc. This is in a French work. One who knows something of the perplexities of exact science, of the mistakes and daily confessions of her staff, feels inclined, after reading such pompous stuff, to exclaim with the malcontent of the Bible: *Tradidit mundum ut non sciant.* Verily—"the world was delivered to them that *they should never know* it."

How likely the scientists are *to succeed* in this direction may be inferred from the fact that the great Humboldt himself could give expression to such erroneous axioms as this one: "Science begins for man only *when his mind has mastered* Matter!"[2] The word "spirit" for "matter" might perhaps have expressed a greater truth. But E. Renan would not have complimented the venerable author of the *Kosmos* in the terms he did, had the term matter been replaced by spirit.

I intend to give a few illustrations to show that the knowledge of matter alone, with the quondam "imponderable" force—whatever the adjective may have meant with the French Academy and Royal Society at the time it was invented—is not sufficient for the purposes of true science. Nor will it ever prove efficient to explain the simplest phenomenon even in objective physical nature, let alone the abnormal cases in which physiologists and biologists at present manifest such interest. As Father Secchi, the famous Roman astronomer expressed it in his work,[3] "if but a few of the *new* forces

---

[2] *Kosmos*, Vol. I, pp. 3 and 76 (with same ideas).
[3] *L'unità delle Forze Fisiche.*

were proven, they would necessitate the admission in space of agents of *quite another order* than those of gravitation."

"I have read a great deal about occultism and studied Kabbalistic books: I have never understood one word in them!"—was a recent remark made by a learned experimenter in "thought-transference," "colour-sounds," and so on.

Very likely. One has to study his letters before he can spell and read, or understand what he reads.

Some forty years back, I knew a child—a little girl of seven or eight—who very seriously frightened her parents by saying:

"Now, mama, I love you. You are good and kind to me to-day. Your words *are quite blue*"...

"What do you mean?"... asked the mother.

"Your words are all blue—because they are so caressing, but when you scold me *they are red* ... so red! But it is worse when you fly in a passion with papa for then they are orange ... horrid ... like that"...

And the child pointed to the hearth, with a big roaring fire and huge flames in it. The mother turned pale.

After that the little sensitive was heard very often associating sounds with colours. The melody played by the mother on the piano threw her into ecstasies of delight; she saw "such beautiful rainbows," she explained, but when her aunt played, it was "fireworks and stars, brilliant stars *shooting pistols*—and then . . . bursting" . . .

The parents got frightened and suspected that something had gone wrong with the child's brain. The family physician was sent for.

"Exuberance of childish fancy," he said. "Innocent hallucinations. . . Don't let her drink tea, and make her play more with her little brothers—fight with them, and have physical exercise. . . ."

And he departed.

In a large Russian city, on the banks of the Volga, stands an hospital with a lunatic asylum attached to it. There a poor woman was locked up for over twenty years—to the day of her death in fact—as a "harmless" though *insane* patient. No other proofs of her insanity could be found on the case-books than the fact that the splash and murmur of the river-waves produced the finest "God's rainbows" for her; while the voice of the superintendent caused her to see "black and crimson"—the *colours of the Evil one.*

About that same period, namely in 1840, something similar to this phenomenon was heralded by the French papers. Such an abnormal state of feelings—physicians thought in those days—could be due but to one reason; such *impressions* whenever experienced without any *traceable* cause, denoted an ill-balanced mind, a weak brain—likely to lead its possessor to lunacy. Such was *the decree* of science. The views of the piously inclined, supported by the affirmations of the village *curés*, inclined the other way. The brain had nought to do with the "obsession" for it was simply the work or tricks of the much slandered "old gentleman" with cloven foot and shining horns. Both the men of learning and the superstitious "good women" have had somewhat to alter their opinions since 1840.

Even in that early period and before the "Rochester" wave of spiritualism had swept over any considerable portion of civilized society in Europe, it was shown that the same phenomenon could be produced by means of various narcotics and drugs. Some bolder people, who feared neither a charge of lunacy nor the unpleasant prospect of being regarded as wards in "Old Nick's Chancery," made experiments and declared the results publicly. One was Théophile Gautier, the famous French author

Few are those acquainted with the French literature of that day, who have not read the charming story told by that author, in which he describes the dreams of an opium-eater. To analyse the *impressions* at first hand, he took a large dose of *hashish*.

"My hearing" he writes, "acquired marvellous capacities: *I heard the music of the flowers*; sounds—green, red and blue—poured into my ears in clearly *perceptible* waves of *smell* and *colour*. A tumbler upset, the creaking of an arm-chair, a word whispered in the lowest tones vibrated and resounded *within me* like so many claps of thunder. At the gentlest contact with objects—furniture or human body—I heard prolonged sounds, sighs like the melodious vibrations of an Æolian harp. . . . . ."⁴

No doubt the powers of human fancy are great; no doubt delusion and hallucination may be generated for a shorter or a longer period in the healthiest human brain either naturally or artificially. But natural phenomena that are not included in that "abnormal" class do exist; and they have at last taken forcible possession even of scientific minds. The phenomena of hypnotism, of thought-transference, of sense-provoking, merging as they do into one another and manifesting their occult existence in our phenomenal world, succeeded finally in arresting the attention of some eminent scientists. Under the leadership of the famous Dr. Charcot, of the Salpêtrière Hospital in Paris, several famous men of science took the phenomena in hand—in France, Russia, England, Germany and Italy. For over fifteen years they have been experimenting, investigating, theorising. And what is the result? The sole explanation given to the public, to those who thirst to become acquainted with the real, the intimate nature of the phenomena, with their productive cause and genesis—is that the sensitives who manifest them are all hysterical!

They are *psychopates*,[5] and *neurosists*[6]—we are told—no other cause underlying the endless variety of manifestations than that of a purely physiological character.

This looks satisfactory for the present, and—quite hopeful for the future.

---

[4] *La Presse*, July 10, 1840.

[5] A Greek compound term coined by the Russian Medical Faculties.

[6] From the word *neurosis*.

"Hysterical hallucination" is thus doomed to become, as it appears, the *alpha* and the *omega* of every phenomenon. At the same time science defines the word "hallucination" as "an error of our *senses*, shared by, and imposed (by that error) upon our *intelligence*."[7] Now such *hallucinations* of a sensitive as are objective—the apparition of an "astral body" for instance—are not only perceptible by the sensitive's (or medium's) "*intelligence*," but are likewise shared by the senses of those present. Consequently the natural inference is that all those witnesses are also *hysterical*.

The world is in danger, we see, of being turned, by the end of this century, into one vast lunatic asylum, in which the learned physicians alone would form the *sane* portion of humanity.

Of all the problems of medical philosophy, hallucination seems, at this rate, the most difficult to solve, the most obstinate to get rid of. It could hardly be otherwise, for it is one of the mysterious results of our dual nature, the bridge thrown over the chasm that separates the world of matter from the world of spirit. None but those willing to cross to the other side can appreciate it, or ever recognize the *noumenon* of its phenomena. And without doubt a manifestation is quite disconcerting to anyone who witnesses it for the first time. Proving to the materialist the creative faculty, the *potency* of man's spirit, *naturalising* before the churchman the "miracle," and *supernaturalising*, so to say, the simplest effects of natural causes, *hallucination* cannot be accepted yet for what it really is, and could hardly be forced upon the acceptation of either the materialist or the believing Christian, since one is as strong in his denial as the other is in his affirmation. "Hallucination," says an authority quoted

---

[7] *Dictionnaire Médical.*

by Brierre de Boismont,[8] "is the reproduction of the material sign of the idea." Hallucination, it is said, has no respect for age or for merit; or, if a fatal experience is worth anything—"a physician who would give it too much of his attention or would study it for too long a time and *too seriously*, would be sure to end his career in the ranks of his own patients."

This is an additional proof, that "hallucination" was hardly ever studied "too *seriously*" as self-sacrifice is not quite the most prominent feature of the age. But *if* so catching, why should we not be permitted the bold and disrespectful suggestion that the biologists and physiologists of Dr. Charcot's school, have themselves become *hallucinated* with the rather one-sided scientific idea that such phenomenal hallucinations are all due to *Hysteria?*

However it may be, whether a *collective hallucination* of our medical lights or the impotency of material thought, the simplest phenomenon—of the class *accepted* and verified by men of science in the year 1885—remains as unexplained by them, as it was in 1840.

If, admitting for argument sake, that some of the common herd out of their great reverence—often amounting to *fetich worship*—for science and authority, do accept the dictum of the scientists that every phenomenon, every "abnormal" manifestation, is due to the pranks of *epileptic hysteria*, what shall the rest of the public do? Shall they believe that Mr. Eglinton's *self-moving* slate pencil is also labouring under a fit of the same epilepsy as its medium—even though he *does not touch it?* Or that the prophetic utterances of the seers, the grand inspired apostles of all ages and religions, were

---

[8] *Des Hallucinations*, p. 3.

simply the pathological results of hysteria? Or again that the "miracles" of the Bible, those of Pythagoras, Apollonius and others—belong to the same family of *abnormal* manifestations, as the hallucinations of Dr. Charcot's Mlle. *Alphonsine*—or whatever her name—and her erotic descriptions and her poetry—"in consequence *of the swelling with gases of her great bowel*" (*sic*)? Such a pretension is likely to come to grief. First of all "hallucination" itself, when it is really the effect of a physiological cause, would have to be explained—but *it never has been.* Taking at random some out of the hundreds of definitions by eminent French physicians (we have not those of the English at hand) what do we learn about "hallucinations"? We have given Dr. Brierre de Boismont's "definition," if it can be called one: now let us see a few more.

Dr. Lélut calls it—"a *sensorial* and *perceptive* folly"; Dr. Chomel—"a common illusion of the *sensorium*";[9] Dr. F. Leuret—"an illusion intermediary between sensation and conception" (*Fragments Psychologiques sur la Folie*); Dr. Michéa—"a perceptive delirium "(*Du Délire des Sensations*); Dr. Calmeil—"an illusion due to a vicious modification of the nervous substance" (*De la Folie*, Vol. I); etc., etc.

The above will not make the world, I am afraid, much wiser than it is. For my part, I believe the theosophists would do well to keep to the old definition of hallucinations (*theophania*)[10] and folly, made some two thousands of years back by Plato, Virgilius, Hippocrates, Galen and the medical and theological schools of old. "There are two kinds of folly, one of which is produced by the body, the other sent to us *by the gods.*"

---

[9] See *Dictionary of Medical Terms.*
[10] Communication with Gods.

About ten years ago, when *Isis Unveiled* was being written, the most important point the work aimed at was the demonstration of the following: (*a*) the reality of the *Occult* in nature; (*b*) the thorough knowledge of, and familiarity with, all such occult domains amongst "certain men," and their mastery therein; (*c*) hardly an art or science known in our age, that the *Vedas* have not mentioned; and (*d*) that hundreds of things, especially, mysteries of nature—*in abscondito* as the alchemists called it—were known to the Aryas of the *pre-mahabharata* period, which are unknown to us, the modern sages of the 19th century.

A new proof of it is now being given. It comes as a fresh corroboration from some recent investigations in France by learned "*specialists*" (?) with regard to the confusion made by their *neurosists* and *psychomaniacs* between colour and sound, "*musical impressions*" and *colour impressions*.

This special phenomenon was first approached in Austria in 1873 by Dr. Nüssbaumer. After him it began to be seriously investigated in Germany by Bleuler and Lehmann; in Italy by Velardi, Bareggi and a few others, and it was finally and quite recently taken up by Dr. Pedrono of France. The most interesting accounts of *colour-sound* phenomena may, however, be found in *La Nature* (No. 626, [May 30,] 1885, p. 406 et seq.), in an article contributed by A. de Rochas who experimented with a certain gentleman whom he names "N. R."

The following is a short *résumé* of his experience.

N. R. is a man of about 57 years of age, an *advocate* by profession, now living in one of the country *faubourgs* of Paris, a passionate amateur of natural sciences which he has studied very seriously, fond of music, though no musician himself, a great traveller and as great a linguist. N. R. had never read anything about that peculiar phenomenon that makes certain people associate sound with colour, but was subject to it from his very boyhood. Sound of every description had always generated in him the impression of colours. Thus the articulation of the vowels produces in his brain the following results:—The letter *A*—appears to him dark red; *E*—white; *I*—black; *O*—yellow; *U*—blue. The double-vowelled letters: *Ai*—chestnut colour; *Ei*—greyish white; *Eu*—light blue; *Oi*—dirty-yellow; *Ou*—yellowish. The consonants are nearly all of a dark grey hue; while a vowel, or a double vowel forming with a consonant a syllable, colours that syllable with its own tint. Thus, *ba, ca, da* are all of red-grey colour; *bi, ci, di*—ash coloured; *bo, co, do*—yellow grey, and so on. *S* ending a word and pronounced in a hissing way, like the Spanish words *los campos*, imparts to the syllable that precedes it a metallic glittering. The colour of the word depends thus on the colour of the letters that compose it, so that to N. R. human speech appears in the shape of many-coloured, or variegated ribbons coming out of persons' mouths, the colours of which are determined by those of the vowels in the sentences, separated one from the other by the greyish stripes of the consonants.

The languages receive in their turn a common colouring from those letters that predominate in each. For instance, the German, which abounds in consonants, forms on the whole the impression of a dark grey moss; French appears grey, strongly mixed with white; the English seems nearly black; Spanish is very much coloured especially with yellow and carmin-red tints; Italian is yellow, merging into carmin and black, but with more delicate and harmonious tints than the Spanish.

A deep-toned voice impresses N. R. with a dark red colour which gradually passes into a chocolate hue; while a shrill, sonorous voice suggests the blue colour, and a voice between these two extremes changes these colours immediately into very light yellow.

The sounds of instruments have also their distinct and special colours: the piano and the flute suggest tints of blue; the violin—black; and the guitar—silver grey, etc.

The names of musical notes pronounced loudly, influence N. R. in the same manner as the words. The colours of a singing voice and playing depend upon the voice and its compass and altitude, and upon the instrument played on.

So it is with *figures* verbally pronounced; but when read mentally they reflect for him the colour of the ink they are written or printed with. The form, therefore, has nought to do with such colour phenomena. While these impressions do not generally take place outside of himself, but perform, so to say, on the platform of his brain, we find other sensitives offering far more curious phenomena than "N. R." does.

Besides Galton's interesting chapter upon this subject, in his "Inquiries into human faculty and its development," we find in the *London Medical Record* a sensitive describing his impressions in this wise: "As soon as I *hear* the sounds of a guitar, I *see* vibrating chords, surrounded by coloured vapours." The piano produces the same: "coloured images begin to float over the keys." One of Dr.

Pedrono's subjects in Paris[11] has always colour impressions *outside* of himself. "Whenever I hear a chorus composed of several voices," he says, "I *feel* a great number of coloured points floating over the heads of the singers. I *feel* them, for my eye receives no definite impression; nevertheless, I am compelled to *look* at them and while *examining* them I feel perplexed, for I cannot find those bright coloured spots where I *look* at them, or rather *feel* them."

Inversely, there are sensitives in whom the sight of colours evokes immediately that of sounds, and others again, in whom a triple phenomenon is produced by one special sense generating two other senses. A certain sensitive cannot hear a brass band without a taste "like copper in the mouth" during the performance, and seeing dark golden clouds.

Science investigates such manifestations, recognizes their reality, and—remains powerless to explain them. "*Neurosis* and *hysteria*" is the only answer obtained, and the "*canine* hallucinations" of the French academicians quoted in *Isis*, have remained valid to this day as an explanation, or a *universal solvent* of all such phenomena. But it is only natural after all, that science should be unable to account at any rate for this particular phenomenon of *light* and *sound*, since its theory of light itself has never been fully verified, nor made complete to the present day.

Let then our scientific opponents play for a while longer at "blindman's buff" amongst phenomena, with no ground to stand upon but their eternal physiological hypotheses. The time is not

---

[11] *Annales d'Oculistique*, Nov. and Dec., 1882.—*Journal de Médecine de l'Ouest*, 4me Trimestre, 1882.

perhaps far off when they shall be compelled to change their tactics or—confess themselves defeated by even such *elementary* phenomena as described above. But, whatever physiologists may, or may not say, or do; whatever their scientific explanations, hypotheses and conclusions at present or in the future, modern phenomena are fast *cycling* back for their true explanation, to the archaic *Vedas*, and other "Sacred Books of the East." For it is an easy matter to show, that the Vedic Aryans were quite familiar with all such mysteries of sound and colour. *Mental* correlations of the two senses of "sight" and "hearing " were as common a fact in their days, as that of a man in our own seeing objective things before him with his eyes wide open at noon.

Any student of Occultism, the youngest of *chelas* who has just begun reading *esoterically* his Vedas, can suspect what the real phenomenon means; simply—*a cyclic return of human organisms to their primitive form* during the 3rd and even the 4th Root Races of what is known as the *Antediluvian periods*. Everything conspires to prove it, even the study of such exact sciences as philology and comparative mythology. From the hoary days of antiquity, from the very dawn of the grand civilizations of those races that preceded our *Fifth* Race, and the traces of which now lie buried at the very bottom of the oceans, the fact in question was known. That which is now considered as an abnormal phenomenon, was in every probability the normal state of the antediluvian Humanity. These are no vain words, for here are two of the many proofs.

In consequence of the abundant data gleaned by linguistic research, philologists are beginning to raise their voices and are pointing to some very suggestive, though as yet unexplained facts. (1) All the words indicative of human representations and conceptions of *light* and *sound* are *found to have their derivation from the same roots.*[12] (*2*) *Mythology* shows, in her turn, the evident law—the uniformity of which precludes the possibility of chance—that led the ancient symbologists to represent all their *sun-*gods and *radiant* deities—such as the Dawn, the Sun, Aurora, Phoebus, Apollo, etc.—connected in one way or the other with music and singing—with *sound* in short—associated with radiancy and colour.[13]

If this is as yet but an inference, there exists a still better proof in the *Vedas*, for there the conceptions of the words "sound" and "light," "to hear" and "to see," *are always associated.* In Hymn X, 71, verse 4, we read: "One—though *looking, sees not the speech,* and the other *seeing*—does not *hear* it." And again in verse 7th, in which a party of friends is represented as emulating each other in singing, they are charactered by the double epithet placed side by side: *Akshavanta* and *Karnavanta*, or "one furnished with eyes" and "one furnished with ears." The latter is natural—the singer has *a good ear for music,* and the epithet is comprehensible in view of the musical emulation. But what sense can the *Akshavanta* have in this case, with his good sight, unless there is a connection and a meaning in it that are not explained, because probably the hymn refers to days when *sight* and *hearing* were synonymous terms? Moreover, a philologist, a rising Orientalist, tells[14] us that " the Sanskrit verbal root *arc* is used to denote two meanings—(*a*) 'to *sing*,' and (*b*) 'to *shine*,' to radiate beams or rays. The substantives *rc* and *arka*, derived from the root *arc*, are used to signify (1) *song, hymn,* and (2) *brilliancy,* ray, sun. . . . In the conception of the ancients *a speech could be seen . . .* ," he explains. What does the Esoteric Doctrine,—

---

[12] *Introduction à la mythologie de l'Odyssée*, Voyevodsky.

[13] *Essay on the Bacchic Cults of the Indo-European Nations.*

[14] Professor D. N. Ovsyaniko-Kulikovsky, the Author of the Essay on "Bacchic Cults."

that universal solvent indeed of all scientific difficulties and puzzles—–say to this? It sends us to the chapter on the *Evolution of Races*, in which primitive man is shown in his special evolution advancing on the physical plane by developing a sense in each successive sub-race (of which there are seven) of the 1st Root-race during the 4th Round on this globe.[15] *Human* speech, as known to us, came into being in the Root-race that preceded ours—the *Fourth* or the "Atlantean"—at the very beginning of it, in sub-race No. 1; and simultaneously with it were developed *sight*—as a physical sense—while the four other senses (with the two additional—the 6th and 7th—of which science knows nothing as yet)—remained in their latent, undeveloped state as physical senses, although fully developed as spiritual faculties. Our sense of *hearing* developed only in the 3rd sub-race. Thus, if human "speech"—owing to that absence of the sense of hearing—was in the beginning even less than what we would call a whispered speech, for it was a mental articulation of sounds rather than anything else, something like the systems we now see worked out for the Deaf and Dumb, still it is easy to understand how, even from those early days, "speech" became associated with "sight," or, in other words, people could understand each other and *talk* with the help of only *sight* and *touch*. "Sound is *seen* before it is heard"—says the *Book of Kiu-ti*. The flash of lightning precedes the clap of thunder. As ages went by mankind fell with every new generation lower and lower *into matter*, the physical smothering the spiritual, until the whole set of senses—that had formed during the first three Root-races but one Sense, namely, *spiritual perception*—finally fell asunder to form henceforth five distinct senses.

---

[15] See *Esoteric Buddhism*—for the Rounds, World-periods, and Subraces. The chapter referred to will appear in *The Secret Doctrine*, which will shortly be published.

But we are in the 5th race, and we have already passed the turning or *axial* point of our "sub-race cycle." Eventually as the current phenomena and the increase of sensitive organisms in our age go to prove, this Humanity will be moving swiftly on the path of pure spirituality, and will reach the apex (of *our* Race) at the end of the 7th sub-race. In plainer and *fuller* language—*plainer* and *fuller* to some theosophists only, I am afraid—we shall be, at that period, on the same degree of spirituality that belonged to, and was natural in, the 1st sub-race of the 3rd *Root-race* of the Fourth Round; and the second half of it (or that half in which we now are) will be, owing to the law of correspondence, on parallel lines with the *first* half of the Third Round. In the words of one in whom live Truth and Wisdom—however often His words may have been misunderstood and criticised, not alone by profane critics but even by some theosophists—"in the 1st half of the 3rd Round the primordial spirituality of man was eclipsed, because over-shadowed by nascent mentality"; Humanity was on its *descending arc* in the first half of that round and in the last half on its ascending arc: *i.e.*, " his (man's) *gigantic* stature had decreased and his body improved in texture; and he had become a more rational being though still more an ape than a *Deva-man*." And, if so, then, according to that same law of correspondences—an immutable one in the system of cycles—we have to infer the following:—that the latter half of our Round—as shown to correspond with the 1st half of the 3rd,—must have already begun to be once more overshadowed by renascent "primordial" spirituality, which, at the end of the 4th Round, will have nearly eclipsed our actual mentality—in the sense of cold *human* Reason.

On the principle of that same law of correspondences—as shall be shown and thoroughly explained in the forthcoming *Secret Doctrine*—civilized humanity will soon begin to show itself, if even less "rational" *on the worldly plane*, at any rate more *Deva*-like than "ape-like"—as we now actually are, and that in the most distressing degree.

I may conclude with the remark, that since our natural and still "ape-like" propensities make us dread, individually and collectively, to be thrown by public opinion out of that region where all the smaller bodies gravitate toward the luminary of our social solar system—Science and her authority—something has to be done to remedy such a disastrous state of things. I propose to show therefore, in my next, that as we are still only in the 5th subrace of the Parent race, and none of us shall live to see the 7th—when things shall mend naturally,—that it is just as well not to hang our hopes on science, whether orthodox or semi-heretical. The men of science cannot help the world to understand the *rationale* of phenomena, which for a little while longer in this cycle it will be quite impossible for them to account for, even to themselves. They can neither understand nor explain it, any more than anyone else can, who has not studied occultism and the hidden laws that govern nature and rule mankind. The men of science are *helpless* in this case, and it is unjust to charge them with malice, or even with unwillingness—as has been often done. Their *rationality* (taken in this case in the sense of *intellectuality*, not of *reason*) can never permit them to turn their attention to occult study. Therefore it is useless to demand or expect from the learned men of our age that which they are absolutely incapable of doing for us, until the next cycle changes and transforms entirely their *inner* nature by "improving the texture" of their spiritual minds.

PART II

It has already been remarked that neither the medical faculties, nor the scientific bodies of physicists, could ever explain the *primum mobile* or *rationale* of the simplest phenomenon, outside of purely physiological causes; and that, unless they turned for help to occultism, they would have to bite the dust before the 20th century was very old.

This seems a bold assertion. Nevertheless, it is fully justified by that of certain medical celebrities: that *no phenomenon is possible outside of physiological and purely physical causes*. They might reverse this statement and say *no final investigation is possible with the light of only physiological and physical causes*. That would be correct. They might add that, as men of exact science, they could not employ other methods of investigation. Therefore, having conducted their experiments to a certain boundary, they would desist and declare *their* task accomplished. Then the phenomena might be passed on to transcendentalists and philosophers to speculate upon. Had they spoken in such a spirit of sincerity no one would have the right of saying that they had not done their duty: for they would have done the best they could under the circumstances, and, as will presently be shown, they could do no more. But at present the neuropathic physicians merely impede the progress of real psychological knowledge. Unless there is an opening, however small, for the passage of a ray from a man's higher *self* to chase the darkness of purely material conceptions from the seat of his intellect, and to replace it by light from a plane of existence entirely unknown to the ordinary senses, his task can never be wrought to a successful termination. And as all such abnormal cases, in order to be manifested to our physical as well as spiritual senses, in other words, to become objective, must always have their generating causes interblended between the two spheres or planes of existence, the physical and the spiritual, it is but natural that a materialist should discern only those with which he is acquainted, and remain blind to any other.

The following illustration will make this clear to every intellectual reader.

When we speak of light, of heat and sound, and so on, what do we mean? Each of these natural phenomena exists *per se*. But for us it has no being independently of our senses, and exists only to that degree which is perceived by a sense corresponding to it in us. Without being in the least deaf or blind, some men are endowed with far less acute hearing and sight than their neighbours; and it is a well known fact that our senses can be developed and trained as well as our muscles by exercise and method. It is an old axiom that the sun needs an eye to manifest its light; and though the solar energy exists from the first flutter of our Manvantara and will exist to the first killing breath of Pralaya, still, if a certain portion of that energy did not call forth in us those modifications that we name perception of light, Cymmerian darkness would fill the Kosmos and we should be denying the very existence of the sun. Science makes a distinction between the two energies—that of heat and that of light. But the same science teaches us that the creature, or being, in which the corresponding external actions would cause a homogeneous modification, could not find any difference between heat and light. On the other hand, that the creature, or being, in which the dark rays of the solar spectrum would call forth the modifications that are produced in us by the bright rays, would see light there, where we saw nothing whatever.

Mr. A. Butleroff, a professor of chemistry and an eminent scientist, gives us many instances of the above. He points to the observations made by Sir John Lubbock on the sense of colour in ants. It was found by that distinguished man of science, that ants do not allow their eggs to remain subjected to light, and carry them off immediately from a sun-lit spot to a dark place. But when a ray of *red* light is turned on those eggs (the larvæ), the ants leave them untouched as though they were in complete darkness: they place their eggs indifferently under a red light or in utter darkness. Red light is a non-existent thing for them: as they do not see it, it is for them darkness. The impressions made on them by bright rays are very weak, especially by those nearest to the red—the orange and yellow. To such rays, on the contrary, as light and dark blue and violet—they seem very impressionable. When their nests are lit partly with violet and partly with red rays, they transfer their eggs immediately from the violet onto the red field. To the ant, therefore, the violet ray is the brightest of all the spectral rays. Their sense of colour is therefore quite the opposite of the same sense in man.

But this contrast is still more strengthened by another fact. Besides the rays of light, the solar spectrum contains, as everyone knows, the so-called heat rays (for red) and the chemical (for violet). We see however neither the one nor the other, but term both of them *dark rays:* while the ants perceive them clearly. For, as soon as their eggs are subjected to the action of those dark rays, the ants drag them from that (to us) quite obscure field onto the one lighted by the *red* rays: therefore, for them, *the chemical ray is violet.* Hence says the professor—

"Owing to such a peculiarity, the objects seen by the ants must appear to them quite different from what they seem to us; those insects find evidently in nature hues and colours of which we have not, nor can have, the slightest conception. Admit for one moment the existence in nature of such objects as would swallow up all the rays of the solar spectrum, and scatter only the chemical rays: these objects would *remain invisible to us*, while the ants would perceive them very well."

And now, let the reader imagine for one moment the following: that there may be a possibility within the powers of man, with the help of secret sciences, firstly of preparing an "object" (call it *talisman* if you will) which, detaining for a longer or shorter period the rays of the "solar spectrum" on some one given point, will cause the manipulator of it to remain invisible to all, because he places himself and keeps within the boundary of the chemical "dark" rays; and *secondly*—reversing it, to become enabled to see in nature by the help of those dark rays that which ordinary men, with no such "talisman" at hand, can never see with their natural, naked eye! This may be a simple supposition, or it may be a very serious statement, for all the men of science know. They protest only against that which is claimed to be supernatural, above or outside *their* Nature; they have no right to object to the acceptance of the supersensuous, if shown within the limits of our sensuous world.

The same holds good in acoustics. Numerous observations have shown that ants are completely deaf to the sounds that we hear; but that is no reason why we should suppose that ants are deaf. Quite the reverse; for taking his stand on his numerous observations, the same scientist thinks it necessary to accept that the ants hear sounds, "only not those that are perceptible to us."

Every organ of hearing is sensitive to vibrations of a given rapidity, but in cases of different creatures such rapidities may very easily not coincide. And not only in the case of creatures quite different from us men, but even in that of mortals whose organizations are peculiar—*abnormal* as they are termed—either naturally, or through training.[16] Our *ordinary* ear, for instance, is insensible to vibrations surpassing 38,000 a second, whereas the auditive organ of not only ants but some mortals likewise—*who know the way to secure the tympanum from damage, and that of provoking certain correlations in ether*—may be very sensitive to vibrations exceeding by far the 38,000 in a second, and thus, such an auditive organ,—*abnormal* only in the limitations of exact science,—might naturally enable its possessor, whether man or ant, to enjoy sounds and melodies in nature, of which the ordinary tympanum gives no idea. "There, where to our senses reigns dead silence, a thousand of the most varied and weird sounds may be gratifying to the hearing of ants," says Professor Butleroff,[17] citing Lubbock; "and these tiny, intelligent sects could, therefore, regard us with the same right as we have to regard them—as deaf, and utterly incapable of enjoying the music of nature, only because they remain insensible to the sound of a gun, human shouting, whistling, and so on."

The aforesaid instances sufficiently show that the scientist's knowledge of nature is incapable of coinciding wholly and entirely with all that exists and may be found in it. Even without trespassing on other and different spheres and planets, and keeping strictly within the boundaries of our globe, it becomes evident that there exist in it thousands upon thousands of things unseen, unheard, and impalpable to the ordinary human senses. But let us admit, only for the sake of argument, that there may be—quite apart from the supernatural—a science that teaches mortals what may be termed

---

[16] The case of Kashmiri natives and especially girls who work on shawls is given in *Isis*. They perceive 300 hues more than Europeans do.
[17] *Scientific Letters*, X.

supersensuous chemistry and physics; in plainer language—*alchemy* and the *metaphysics* of *concrete* not abstract nature, and every difficulty will be removed. For, as the same Professor argues—

"If we see light there, where another being is plunged in darkness; and see *nothing* there, where it experiences the action of the light waves; if we hear one kind of sounds and remain deaf to another kind of sounds, heard, nevertheless, by a tiny insect—is it not as clear as day, that it is not nature, in her, so to say, primeval nakedness, that is subject to our science and its analysis, but simply those modifications, feelings and perceptions that she awakens in us? It is in accordance with these modifications only that we can draw our conclusions about external things and nature's actions, and thus create to ourselves the image of the world surrounding us. The same, with respect to every 'finite' being: each judging of the external, only by the modifications that are created in him (or it) by the same.

And this, we think, is the case with the materialist: he can judge psychic phenomena only by their external aspect, and no modification is, or ever can be, created in him, so as to open his insight to their spiritual aspect. Notwithstanding the strong position of those several eminent men of science who, becoming convinced of the actuality of "spiritual" phenomena, so-called, have become spiritualists; notwithstanding that—like Professors Wallace, Hare, Zöllner, Wagner, Butleroff—they have brought to bear upon the question all the arguments their great knowledge could suggest to them—their opponents have had, so far always the best of them. Some of these do not deny the fact of phenomenal occurrences but they maintain that the chief point in the great dispute between the transcendentalists of spiritualism and the materialists is simply the nature of the *operative force*, the *primum mobile* of the power at work.

They insist on this main point: the spiritualists are unable to prove that this agency is that of *intelligent spirits of departed human beings*, "so as to *satisfy the requirements of exact science*, or of the unbelieving public for the matter of that." And, viewed from this aspect, their position is impregnable.

The theosophical reader will easily understand that it is immaterial whether the denial is to the title of "spirits" pure and simple or to that of any other intelligent being, whether human, sub-human, or super-human, or even to a Force—if it is unknown to, and rejected *a priori* by science. For it seeks precisely to limit such manifestations to those forces only that are within the domain of natural sciences. In short, it rejects point blank the possibility of showing them mathematically to be that which the spiritualists claim them to be, insisting that they have been already demonstrated.

It becomes evident, therefore, that the Theosophist, or rather the Occultist, must find his position far more difficult than even the spiritualist ever can, with regard to modern science. For it is not to phenomena *per se* that most of the men of science are averse, but to the nature of the agency said to be at work. If, in the case of "Spiritual" phenomena these have only the materialists against them, not so in our case. The theory of "Spirits" has only to contend against those who do not believe in the survival of man's soul. Occultism raises against itself the whole legion of the Academies; because, while putting every kind of "Spirits," good, bad and indifferent, in the second place, if not entirely in the background, it dares to deny several of the most vital scientific dogmas; and in this case, the Idealists and the Materialists of Science, feel equally indignant; for both, however much they may disagree in personal views, serve under the same banner. There is but one science, even though there are two distinct schools—the *idealistic* and the *materialistic*; and both of these are equally considered authoritative and *orthodox* in questions on science. Few are those among us who clamoured for a scientific opinion expressed upon Occultism, who have thought of this, or realized its importance in this respect. Science, unless remodelled entirely, can have no hand in occult teachings. Whenever investigated on the plan of the modern scientific methods, occult phenomena will prove ten times more difficult to explain than those of the spiritualists pure and simple.

It is, after following for nearly ten years, the arguments of many learned opponents who battled for and against phenomena, that an attempt is now being made to place the question squarely before the Theosophists. It is left with them, after reading what I have to say to the end, to use their judgment in the matter, and to decide whether there can remain one tittle of hope for us ever to obtain in that quarter, if not efficient help, at any rate a fair hearing in favour of the Occult Sciences. From none of their members—I say—not even from those whose inner sight has compelled them to accept the reality of the mediumistic phenomena.

This is but natural. Whatever they be, they are men of the modern science even before they are spiritualists, and if not all, some of them at any rate would rather give up their connection with, and belief in, mediums and spirits, than certain of the great dogmas of orthodox, exact science. And they would have to give up not a few of these were they to turn Occultists and approach the threshold of THE MYSTERY in a right spirit of enquiry.

It is this difficulty that lies at the root of the recent troubles of Theosophy; and a few words upon the subject will not be out of season, the more so as the whole question lies in a nut-shell. Those Theosophists who are not Occultists cannot help the investigators, let alone the men of science. Those who are Occultists work on certain lines that *they dare not trespass*. Their mouth is closed; their explanations and demonstrations are limited. What can they do? Science will never be satisfied with a half-explanation.

To know, to dare, to will and to remain silent—is so well known as the motto of the Kabbalists, that to repeat it here may perhaps seem superfluous. Still it may act as a reminder. As it is, we have either said *too much*, or *too little*. I am very much afraid it is the former. If so, then we have atoned for it, for we were the first to suffer for saying *too much*. Even that little might have placed us in worse difficulties hardly a quarter of a century ago.

Science—I mean Western Science—has to proceed on strictly defined lines. She glories in her powers of observation, induction, analysis and inference. Whenever a phenomenon of an abnormal nature comes before her for investigation, she has to sift it to its very bottom, or let it go. And this she has to do, and she cannot, as we have shown, proceed on any other than the inductive methods based entirely on the evidence of physical senses. If these, aided by the scientific *acumen*, do not prove equal to the task, the investigators will resort to, and will not scruple to use, the police of the land, as in the historical cases of Loudun, Salem Witchcraft, Morzine, etc.: The Royal Society calling in Scotland Yard, and the French Academy her native *mouchards*, all of whom will, of course, proceed in their own detective-like way to help science out of difficulty. Two or three cases of "an extremely suspicious character" will be chosen, on the external plane of course, and the rest proclaimed of no importance, as contaminated by those selected. The testimony of eye-witnesses will be rejected, and the evidence of ill-disposed persons speaking on hearsay accepted as "unimpeachable." Let the reader go over the 20 odd volumes of de Mirville's and des Mousseaux's works, embracing over a century of forced enquiry into various phenomena by science, and he will be better able to judge the ways in which scientific, often honourable, men-proceed in such cases.

What can be expected then, even from the *idealistic* school of science, whose members are in so small a minority. Laborious students they are, and some of them open to every truth and without equivocation. Even though they may have no personal *hobbies* to lose, should their previous views be shown to err, still there are such dogmas in orthodox science that even they would *never dare to trespass*. Such, for instance, are their axiomatic views upon the law of gravitation and the modern conceptions of Force, Matter, Light, etc., etc.

At the same time we should bear in mind the actual state of civilized Humanity, and remember how its cultured classes stand in relation to any idealistic school of thought, apart from any question of occultism. At the first glance we find that two-thirds of them are honeycombed with what may be called gross and practical materialism.

"The theoretical materialistic science recognizes nought but Substance. Substance is its deity, its only God." We are told that practical materialism, on the other hand, concerns itself with nothing that does not lead directly or indirectly to personal benefit. "Gold is its idol," justly observes Professor Butleroff[18] (a spiritualist,

---

[18] *Scientific Letters*, X.

yet one who could never accept even the elementary truths of occultism, for he "cannot understand them").

"A lump of matter," he adds, "the beloved substance of the theoretical materialists, is transformed into a lump of mud in the unclean hands of ethical materialism. And if the former gives but little importance to inner (psychic) states that are not perfectly demonstrated by their exterior states, the latter disregards entirely the inner states of life. . . . . The spiritual aspect of life has no meaning for practical materialism, everything being summed up for it in the external. The adoration of this external finds its principal and basic justification in the dogma of materialism, which has legalized it."

This gives the key to the whole situation. Theosophists or Occultists at any rate, have nothing then to expect from materialistic Science and Society.

Such a state of things being accepted for the daily *routine* of life—though that which interferes with the highest moral aspirations of Humanity cannot we believe live long—what can we do but look forward with our hopes to a better future? Meanwhile, we ought never to lose courage; for if materialism, which has depopulated heaven and the elements, and has chosen to make of the limitless Kosmos instead of an eternal abode a dark and narrow tomb, refuses to interfere with us, we can do no better than leave it alone.

Unfortunately it does not. No one speaks so much as the materialists of the accuracy of scientific observation, of a proper use of one's senses and one's reason thoroughly liberated from every prejudice. Yet, no sooner is the same privilege claimed in favour of phenomena by one who has investigated them in that same scientific spirit of impartiality and justice, than his testimony becomes worthless. "Yet if such a number of scientific minds," writes Prof. Butleroff "accustomed by years of training to the minutest observation and verification, testify to certain facts, then there is a *prima facie* improbability that they should be collectively mistaken." "But they *have* and in the most ludicrous way," answer his opponents; and this time we are at one with them.

This brings us back to an old axiom of esoteric philosophy: *"nothing of that which does not exist somewhere, whether in the visible or invisible kosmos, can be reproduced artificially, or even in human thought."*

"What nonsense is this?" exclaimed a combative Theosophist upon hearing it uttered. "Suppose I think of an animated tower, with rooms in it and a human head, approaching and talking with me—can there be such a thing in the universe?"

"Or parrots hatching out of almond-shells?" said an-other sceptic. Why not?—was the answer—not on this earth, of course. But how do we know that there may not be such beings as you describe—tower-like bodies and human heads—on some other planet Imagination is nothing but the memory of preceding births—Pythagoras tells us. You may yourself have been such a "tower man" for all you know, with rooms in you in which your family found shelter like the little ones of the kangaroo. As for parrots hatching out of almond shells—no one could swear that there was no such thing in nature, in days of old, when evolution gave birth to far more curious monsters. A bird hatching out of the fruit of a tree is perhaps one of those countless words dropped by evolution so many ages ago, that the last whisper of its echo was lost in the Diluvian roar.

"The mineral becomes plant, the plant an animal, an animal man," etc. say the Kabbalists.

Speaking of the evidence and the reliability of senses—even the greatest men of science got caught once upon a time, in not only believing such a thing, but in actually teaching it *as a scientific fact—as it appears.*

"When was that?" was the incredulous question. "Not so far back, after all; some 280 years ago—in England." The strange belief that there was a kind of a sea-fowl that hatched out of a fruit was not limited at the very end of the 16th century to the inhabitants of English sea-port towns only. There was a time when most of the men of science firmly believed it to be a fact, and taught it accordingly. The fruit of certain trees growing on the sea shore—a kind of Magnolia—with its branches dipping generally in the water, had its fruits—as it was asserted—transformed gradually by the action of salt water into some special Crustacean formation, from which emerged in good time a living sea-bird, known in the old natural histories as the "Barnacle-goose." Some naturalists accepted the story as an undeniable fact. They observed and investigated it for several years, and the discovery was accepted and approved by the greatest authorities of the day and published under the auspices of some learned society. One of such believers in the "Barnacle-goose" was John Gerard, a botanist, who notified the world of the amazing phenomenon in an erudite work published in 1596. In it he describes it, and declares it *"a fact on the evidence of his own senses."* "He has seen it himself," he says, " touched the fruit-egg day after day," watched its growth and development personally, and had the good luck of presiding at the birth of one such bird. He saw first the legs of the chicken oozing out through the broken shell, then the whole body of the little Barnacle-goose "which begun forthwith swimming."[19] So much was the botanist convinced of the truth of the whole thing, that he ends his description by inviting any doubter of the reality of what he had seen to come and see him, John Gerard, and then he would undertake to make of him an eye-witness to the whole proceeding. Robert Murray another English *savant* and an authority in his day, vouches for the reality of the transformation of which he was also an eye-witness.[20] And other learned men, the contemporaries of Gerard and Murray—Funck, Aldrovandi, and many others shared that conviction.[21] So what do you say to this "Barnacle-goose"?

—Well, I would rather call it the "Gerard-Murray goose," that's all. And no cause to laugh at such mistakes of those early scientists. Before two hundred years are over our descendants will have far better opportunities to make fun of the present generations of the F.R.S. and their followers. But the opponent of phenomena who quoted the story about the "Barnacle-goose" is quite right there; only that instance cuts both ways, of course, and when one brings it as a proof that even the scientific authorities, who believe in spiritualism and phenomena, may have been grossly mistaken with all their observation and scientific training, we may reverse the weapon and quote it the other way; as an evidence as strong that no

---

[19] From the *Scientific Letters*—Letter XXIV, Against Scientific Evidence in the Question of Phenomena.

[20] He speaks of that transformation in the following words, as translated from the Latin: "In every conch (or shell) that I opened, after the transformation of the fruits on the branches into shells, I found the exact picture in miniature in it of the sea-fowl: a little beak like that of a goose, well dotted eyes; the head, the neck, the breast, the wings, and the already formed legs and feet, with well marked feathers on the tail, of a dark colour, etc., etc."

[21] It is evident that this idea was commonly held in the latter half of the 17th century, seeing that it found a place in *Hudibras*, which was an accurate reflection of the opinions of the day:—
"As barnacles turn Poland Geese
In the islands of the Orchades."—Ed. [Theos.]

"acumen" and support of science can prove a phenomenon "referable to fraud and credulity," when the eye-witnesses who have seen it know it for a fact at least. It only shows that the evidence of even the scientific and well trained senses and powers of observation may be in both cases at fault as those of any other mortal, especially in cases where phenomenal occurrences are sought to be disproved. Even collective observation would go for nought, whenever a phenomenon happens to belong to a plane of being, called (improperly so in their case) by some men of science the fourth dimension of space; and when other scientists who investigate it lack the *sixth sense* in them, that corresponds to that plane.

In a literary cross-firing that happened some years ago between two eminent professors, much was said of that now for ever famous fourth dimension. One of them, telling his readers that while he accepted the possibility of only the "terrestrial natural sciences," *viz.*, the direct or inductive science, "or the exact investigation of those phenomena only which take place in our *earthly conditions of space and time*," says he can never permit himself to overlook the possibilities of the future.

"I would remind my colleagues," adds the Professor-Spiritualist, "that our inferences from that which is already acquired by investigation, must go a great deal further than our sensuous perceptions. The limits of sensuous knowledge must be subjected to constant enlargement, and those of deduction still more. Who shall dare to draw those limits for the future ? . . . . . Existing in a three-dimensional space, we can conduct our investigations of, and make our observations upon, merely that which takes place within those three dimensions. But what is there to prevent us thinking of a space of higher dimensions and building a geometry corresponding to it? . . . . . Leaving the reality of a four-dimensional space for the time being aside, we can still . . . . . go on observing and watching whether there may not be met with occasionally on our three-dimensional world, phenomena that could only be explained on the supposition of a four-dimensional space."

In other words,

"we ought to ascertain whether anything pertaining to the four-dimensional regions can manifest itself in our three-dimensional world . . . . can it not be reflected in it . . . .?"

The occultist would answer, that our senses can most undeniably be reached on this plane, not only from a four-dimensional but even a fifth and sixth-dimensional world. Only those senses must become sufficiently *spiritualized* for it, in so far as it is our inner sense only that can become the medium for such a transmission. Like "the projection of an object that exists in a space of three dimensions can be made to appear on the flat surface of a screen of only two dimensions"—four-dimensional beings and things can be *reflected* in our three-dimensional world of gross matter. But, as it would require a skilful physicist to make his audience believe that the things "real as life" they see on his screen are not shadows but realities, so it would take a wiser one than any of us to persuade a man of science—let alone a crowd of scientific men—that what he sees reflected on our three-dimensional "screen" may be, at times, and under certain conditions, a very real phenomenon, reflected from, and produced by "four-dimensional powers," for his private delectation, and as a means to convince him. "Nothing so false in appearance as naked truth"—is a Kabbalistic saying;—"truth is often stranger than fiction"—is a world-known axiom.

It requires more than a man of our modern science to realize such a possibility as an interchange of phenomena between the two worlds—the visible and the invisible. A highly spiritual, or a very keen impressionable intellect, is necessary to decipher intuitionally the real from the unreal, the natural from the artificially prepared "screen." Yet our age is a reactionary one, hooked on the very end of the Cyclic coil, or what remains of it. This accounts for the flood of phenomena, as also for the blindness of certain people.

What does materialistic science answer to the idealistic theory of a four-dimensional space? "How!" it exclaims, "and would you make us attempt, while circumscribed within the impossible circle of a three-dimensional space, to even think of a space of higher dimensions! But how is it possible to think of that, which our human thought can never imagine and represent even in its most hazy outlines? One need be quite a different being from a human creature; be gifted with quite a different psychic organization; one must not be a man, in short, to find himself enabled to represent in his thought a four-dimensional space, a thing of length, breadth, thickness and—what else?"

Indeed, "what else?"—for no one of the men of science, who advocate it, perhaps only because they are sincere spiritualists and anxious to explain phenomena by the means of that space, seem to know it themselves. Is it the "passage of matter through matter"? Then why should they insist upon it being a "space" when it is simply another *plane of existence*—or at least that is what ought to be meant by it—if it means anything. We occultists say and maintain, that if a name is needed to satisfy the material conceptions of men on our low plane, let them call it by its Hindu name *Mahas* (or Mahaloka)—the fourth world of the higher septenary, and one that corresponds to *Rasatala* (the fourth of the septenary string of the nether worlds)—the fourteen worlds that "sprung from the quintuplicated elements"; for these two worlds are enveloping, so to say, our present fourth-round world. Every Hindu will understand what is meant. *Mahas* is a higher world, or plane of existence rather; as that plane to which belongs the ant just spoken of, is perchance a lower one of the nether septenary chains. And if they call it so—they will be right.

Indeed, people speak of this four-dimensional space as though it were a locality—a sphere instead of being what it is—quite a different state of Being. Ever since it came to be resurrected in people's minds by Prof. Zöllner, it has led to endless confusion. How did it happen? By the means of an abstruse mathematical analysis a spiritual-minded man of science finally came to the laudable conclusion that our conception of space may not be infallible, nor is it absolutely proven that besides our three-dimensional calculations it is mathematically impossible that there are spaces of more or less dimensions in the wide Universe. But, as is well expressed by a sceptic—

"the confession of the possible existence of spaces of different dimensions than our own does not afford us (the high mathematicians) the slightest conception of what those dimensions really are. To accept a higher 'four-dimensional' space is like accepting infinitude: such an acceptation does not afford us the smallest help by which we might represent to ourselves either of these . . . all we know of such higher spaces is, that they have nothing in common with our conceptions of space." (*Scientific Letters*.)

"*Our conception*"—means of course the conception of *materialistic* Science, thus leaving a pretty wide margin for other less scientific, withal more spiritual, minds.

To show the hopelessness of ever bringing a materialistic mind to realize or even conceive in the most remote and hazy way the presence among us, in our three-dimensional world of other higher planes of being, I may quote from the very interesting objections made by one of the two learned opponents,[22] already referred to, with regard to this "Space." He asks:

"Is it possible to introduce as an explanation of certain phenomena the action of such a factor, of which we know nothing certain, are ignorant even of its nature and its faculties?"

Perchance, there are such, who may "know" something, who are not so hopelessly ignorant. If an occultist were appealed to, he would say—"No; *exact* physical science has to reject its very being, otherwise that science would become *metaphysical*. It cannot be analyzed—hence explained, on either biological or even physiological data. Nevertheless, it might, inductively—as *gravitation* for instance, of which you know no more than that its effects may be observed on our three-dimensional earth."

Again (1) "It is said" (by the advocates of the theory) "that we live *unconditionally* in our three-dimensional space! Perchance" (*unconditionally*) "just because we are able to comprehend only such space, and absolutely incapable, owing to our organization, to realize it in any other, but a three-dimensional way!"

---

[22] 1883—*Scientific Letters*—published in the *Novoye Vremya, St. Petersburg.*

(2) In other words, "even our three-dimensional space is not something *existing independently*, but represents merely the product of our understanding and perceptions."

To the first statement Occultism answers that those "incapable to realize" any other space but a three-dimensional one, do well to leave alone all others. But it is not "owing to our (human) organization," but only to the intellectual organization of those who are not able to conceive of any other; to organisms undeveloped spiritually and even mentally in the right direction. To the second statement it would reply, that the "opponent" is absolutely wrong in the first, and absolutely right in the last portion of his sentence. For, though the "fourth dimension"—if we must so call it—exists no more *independently* of our perceptions and senses than our three-dimensional *imagined* space, nor as a locality, it still *is*, and exists for the beings evolved and born in it as "a product of their understanding and *their* perceptions." Nature never draws too harsh lines of demarcation, never builds impassable walls, and her unbridged "chasms" exist merely in the tame conceptions of certain naturalists. The two (and more) "spaces," or planes of being, are sufficiently interblended to allow of a communication between those of their respective inhabitants who are capable of conceiving both a higher and a lower plane. There may be amphibian beings intellectually as there are amphibious creatures terrestrially.

The objector to a fourth-dimensional plane complains that the section of high mathematics, known at present under the name of "Metamathematics," or "Metageometry," is being misused and misapplied by the spiritualists. They "seized hold of, and fastened to it as to an anchor of salvation." His arguments are, to say the least, curious. "Instead of proving the reality of their mediumistic phenomena," he says, "they took to explaining them on the hypothesis of a fourth dimension. Do we see the hand of a Katie King, which disappears in "unknown space"—forthwith on the proscenium—the *fourth* dimension; do we get knots on a rope whose two ends are tied and sealed—again that fourth dimension. From this standpoint space is viewed as something objective. It is believed that there are indeed in nature three, four and five-dimensional spaces. But, firstly, by the means of mathematical analysis, we might arrive, in this way, at an endless series of *spaces*. Only think, what would become of exact sciences, if, to explain phenomena, such hypothetical *spaces* were called to its help. If one should fail, we could evoke another, a still higher one, and so on . . . ."

Oh, poor Kant! And yet we are told that one of his fundamental principles was—that our three-dimensional space is not an absolute one; and that "even in respect to such axioms as those of Euclid's geometry, our knowledge and sciences can only be relatively exact and real."

But why should exact science be thought in danger only because spiritualists try to explain their phenomena on that plane? And on what other could they explain that which is inexplicable if we undertake to analyze it on the three-dimensional conceptions of terrestrial science, if not by the fourth-dimensional conception? No sane man would undertake to explain the *Dæmon* of Socrates by the shape of the great sage's nose, or attribute the inspiration of *The Light of Asia* to Mr. Edwin Arnold's skull cap. What would become of science—verily, were the phenomena left to be explained on the said hypothesis? Nothing worse, we hope, than what became of science, after the Royal Society had accepted its modern theory of *Light*, on the hypothesis of an universal *Ether*. Ether is no less "a product of our understanding" than Space is. And if one could be

47

accepted, then why reject the other? Is it because one can be materialized in our conceptions, or shall we say had to be, since there was no help for it; and that the other, being useless as a hypothesis for the purposes of exact science, is not, so far?

So far as the Occultists are concerned, they are at one with the man of strict orthodox science, when to the offer made "to experiment and to observe whether there may not occur in our three-dimensional world phenomena, explainable only on the hypothesis of the existence of a space of four dimensions," they answer as they do. "Well"—they say—"and shall observation and experiment give us a satisfactory answer to our question concerning the real existence of a higher four-dimensional space? Or, solve for us a dilemma unsolvable from whatever side we approach it? How can our human observation and our human experiments, possible only *unconditionally* within the limits of a space of three dimensions, serve us as a point of departure for the recognition of phenomena which can be explained *"only if we admit the existence of a four-dimensional space?"*

The above objections are quite right we think; and the spiritualists would be the only losers were they to ever prove the existence of such space or its interference in their phenomena. For see, what would happen. No sooner would it be demonstrated that—say, a ring does pass through solid flesh and emigrate from the arm of the medium on to that of the investigator who holds the two hands of the former; or again, that flowers and other material things are brought through closed doors and walls; and that, therefore, owing to certain exceptional conditions, matter can pass through matter—no sooner would the men of science get collectively convinced of the fact, than the whole theory of spirit agency and intelligent intervention would crumple to dust. The three-dimensional space would not be interfered with, for the passage of one solid through the other does nothing to do away with even metageometrical dimensions, but matter would be probably endowed by the learned bodies with one more faculty, and the hands of the materialists strengthened thereby. Would the world be nearer the solution of psychic mystery? Shall the noblest aspirations of mankind after the knowledge of real spiritual existence on those planes of being that are now confused with the "four-dimensional space" be the nearer to solution, because exact science shall have admitted as a physical law the action of one man walking deliberately through the physical body of another man, or through a stone wall? Occult sciences teach us that at the end of the Fourth Race, matter, which evolutes, progresses and changes, as we do along with the rest of the kingdoms of nature, shall acquire its fourth sense, as it acquires an additional one with every new Race. Therefore, to an Occultist there is nothing surprising in the idea that the physical world should be developing and acquiring new faculties,—a simple modification of matter, new as it now seems to science, as incomprehensible as were at first the powers of steam, sound, electricity. . . . But what does seem surprising is the spiritual stagnation in the world of intellect, and of the highest exoteric knowledge.

However, no one can impede or precipitate the progress of the smallest cycle. But perhaps old Tacitus was right: "Truth is established by investigation and delay; falsehood prospers by precipitancy." We live in an age of steam and mad activity, and truth can hardly expect recognition in this century. The Occultist waits and bides his time.

www.ingramcontent.com/pod-product-compliance
Lightning Source LLC
LaVergne TN
LVHW041501070426
835507LV00009B/737